EXPERIENCING COMMUNITY

A PILGRIMAGE
SMALL GROUP GUIDE BY
THOM CORRIGAN

NAVPRESS
BRINGING TRUTH TO LIFE
NavPress Publishing Group
P.O. Box 35001, Colorado Springs, Colorado 80935

The Navigators is an international Christian organization. Our mission is to reach, disciple, and equip people to know Christ and to make Him known through successive generations. We envision multitudes of diverse people in the United States and every other nation who have a passionate love for Christ, live a lifestyle of sharing Christ's love, and multiply spiritual laborers among those without Christ.

NavPress is the publishing ministry of The Navigators. NavPress publications help believers learn biblical truth and apply what they learn to their lives and ministries. Our mission is to stimulate spiritual formation among our readers.

Cover illustration: Ian O'Leary / Tony Stone Images

Pilgrimage small group study guides are published in conjunction with The Pilgrimage Group, an organization that trains pastors and lay leaders across the United States and Canada in the essentials of small group ministry and leadership. For more information on Pilgrimage training or consulting, call 1-800-477-7787. Or, visit the Pilgrimage web site at http//www.pilgrimage.org/training/.

Unless otherwise identified, all Scripture quotations in this publication are taken from the *HOLY BIBLE: NEW INTERNATIONAL VERSION* ® (NIV®), copyright © 1973, 1978, 1984 by International Bible Society, used by permission of Zondervan Publishing House, all rights reserved. Other versions used include: *The Message* (MSG) by Eugene H. Peterson, copyright © 1993, 1994, 1995, 1996, used by permission of NavPress Publishing Group; the *New American Standard Bible* (NASB), © The Lockman Foundation 1960, 1962, 1963, 1968, 1971, 1972, 1973, 1975, 1977, used by permission.

Printed in the United States of America

2 3 4 5 6 7 8 9 10 11 12 13 14 15 / 02 01 00 99 98 97

Contents

How This Study Guide Works

Building Community

The life of following Christ was never meant to be solitary. The early Christians pursued it in groups not much larger than the average small group, meeting in homes for the first two hundred years or so of the movement. By meeting in a small group, you are following a time-tested format for spiritual life.

People join small groups for all sorts of reasons: to know a few people well; to be cared for; to learn; to grow spiritually. We believe small groups are the ideal setting in which people learn what it means to take on the character of Christ, and also to put that knowledge into practice. While there are many helpful things one can do alone or in a large group, a small group offers many advantages. Among other things, group members can:

- ▶ encourage one another in good times and bad
- ▶ ask thoughtful questions when a member has a decision to make
- ▶ listen to God together
- ▶ learn how to pray
- ▶ pray for each other
- ▶ benefit from one another's insights into Scripture
- ▶ acquire a habit of reading the Bible on a regular basis
- ▶ practice loving their neighbors
- ▶ worship God together
- ▶ learn to communicate effectively
- ▶ solve problems together
- ▶ receive care from others
- ▶ experience the pleasure of helping another person grow

It will be a rare group that immediately fulfills all of these goals effectively and develops a level of significant trust. Normally we have to earn one another's trust through the gradual formation of the group. Pilgrimage guides reflect the fact that groups proceed through stages.

Experiencing Community is designed to lay a foundation of solid relationships on which a group can build an ongoing life together. This guide emphasizes relationship-building and helps you explore what it means to be a community of Christ-followers. You will discuss the purpose of your small group; the ground rules on which your group will operate; the way you function together (in light of being members of one body); what loving one another looks like in daily life; and how you can attend both to group needs within and ministry needs outside your group. By the end of these seven sessions, you will have developed a sense of community and will be ready to pursue the purposes you have chosen.

A Modular Approach

Each session is divided into several modules or sections. Suggested times are given for each module so that you can complete the session in 60 to 90 minutes. The modules are:

Overview: The first page of each session briefly describes the objectives for your meeting so that you will know what to expect and what results to strive for. You will also learn something about the author's story as it relates to the topic at hand.

Assignment Debriefing: You will take a few minutes at the beginning of each session to discuss the results of your assignment from the previous session.

Beginning: Building relationships is one of the chief tasks of a new group, and extended time is given for this in the guide. Each session includes several questions to help you learn who the other members are and where they have been in their lives. The beginning questions also help you move from what you were thinking about (or worried about) when you arrived at the meeting to what the biblical text deals with. It puts you in touch with the topic in an experiential way, so that your discussion is not simply about sharing ideas, but sharing life. The questions in this section always focus on life experiences and are usually fun to answer.

The Text: You will examine brief passages from various parts of the Bible. *The Message* by Eugene Peterson is the translation most often used in this guide because Peterson's rendering is deliberately relational, easily accessible to people who have never read the Bible before, and fresh to most readers' ears. Even if the text is familiar, this translation helps you see it with new eyes. Since the New Testament was written to be read aloud, you will begin your study by reading the text aloud. Words in bold type are explained in the Reference Notes section.

Understanding the Text: Unless you notice carefully what the text says, you will not be able to interpret it accurately. The questions in this section will help you to focus on the key issues and to wrestle with what the text means. In this section you will examine the passage in its original first-century context.

Applying the Text: It is not enough simply to understand the passage; you need to apply that understanding to your own situation. The questions in this section connect what you have read to how you should live. Because *Experiencing Community* is designed to help you grow together as a group, the questions focus on your role as a member of this group.

Assignment: Rather than going home to study a Bible passage for your next meeting, you will leave the session with a few simple group-building tasks. Beginning with session 3, your assignment will include jotting down brief notes for yourself on what you learned from the session and what you plan to do about it. If you keep up the habit of maintaining such a journal, you will be able to look back and see how God has led you through this group experience.

Prayer: Praying together can build your faith and your relationships in the group. Since many people have never prayed with others before, the suggestions for group prayer begin gradually.

Reference Notes: In order to understand accurately the meaning of the text, one needs to know a little about the context in which it was written and the key words and phrases the text contains. The notes include background on the characters, information about cultural practices, word definitions, and so on. Words and phrases in the text that are highlighted in bold type will have more information or examination in this section. You can scan the notes after reading the text aloud, or during your discussion of Understanding the Text.

Help for the Leader

This study guide provides everything the leader needs to facilitate the group's discussion. In each session, the icon ❶ indicates instructions for the leader. The appendix that begins on page 69 contains additional information to help a leader launch a new group.

It is important that you as the leader read through this guide before you begin the first session so that you understand the direction this guide will take your group. Then re-read each session before you lead it. You need to know where the group is going and the issues you will discuss and pray about each week.

Remember: A leader leads! You will set the pace for the level of sharing, transparency, and need for prayer.

Finally, please remember the critical element that will make or break your group: your willingness to invite Jesus to be in your midst and to touch group members' hearts.

Answers to Common Questions

Who is this material designed for?

> ▶ Anyone who wants to begin a group of Christ-followers.
> ▶ People who have never been in a group before, as well as those who have been in other groups.
> ▶ People with little or no knowledge of the Bible, as well as those who are well acquainted with it.

What if I don't know much about the Bible?

> ▶ The reference notes should tell you what you need to know to make sense of each Bible text.

Is homework necessary?

> ▶ No, the group can meet with no prior preparation.
> ▶ However, the assignments are a great benefit to your group experience. They are designed to help you apply what you have discussed.

How often should we meet?

> ▶ Once a week is best, but every other week also works well.

How long should we meet?

▶ You'll need at least an hour.
▶ Ninety minutes is best—this gives time for more discussion, prayer, and worship.
▶ If you have only 60 minutes, you may need to compress the Beginning and Applying the Text sections.
▶ Some groups may decide to meet for two hours, especially if you have more than eight people.

How do I form a group?

▶ See the ideas for recruiting members on pages 72-73.

Gathering with Jesus

❶ Agenda: *It's wise to outline your agenda before you meet. Be aware of how much time each agenda item will take. Use the suggested times below as a guideline, but don't let the agenda become too stiff and stifle the group. Make sure you have at least one more chair than the number of people at the meeting (see Assignment). Start on time!*

▼ ▼ ▼ ▼ ▼ ▼ ▼ ▼ ▼ ▼ ▼ ▼ ▼ ▼ ▼ ▼ ▼ ▼

Overview   10 minutes

❶ *Welcome: It's important that you warmly welcome everyone who comes to the first meeting, and to every meeting thereafter. Introduce yourself to the group, sharing:*

- ▶ your name
- ▶ one ordinary fact about yourself ("I have three kids")
- ▶ one unusual fact about yourself ("I won the third grade spelling championship," or "I just published an article in *The New England Journal of Medicine*")

Introduce the host(s) and your apprentice leader, if you have one. Ask the host(s) and apprentice to share an ordinary and an unusual fact about themselves as well.

Next, briefly go over your agenda for the meeting. What should group members expect? Pass out discussion guides if necessary. Then ask someone to read aloud the story that follows:

It's one thing to get together for a meeting. It's quite another to explore the issues involved in becoming a group, and even more, to investigate building Christian community. In this session we will begin to get acquainted with each other by telling some of our "stories." Then we will compare our beginning as a small group with the beginning of Jesus' small group. We hope the session will whet the group's appetite for more small-group experiences.

I have spent most of the last eighteen years recruiting people and overseeing small-group ministry. During all this, my wife, Chris, has hated groups. Even though I have tried to give her space and have not demanded that she participate, I had to ask her once to stop telling people in our church about her great dislike for groups because these comments made me look bad. But recently, Chris finally shared something very personal in a new group. She didn't do this because she felt she had to, or to appease the group. Rather, because she finally felt comfortable letting a few other people into her private space. Some people just take longer than others to warm up to the idea of opening up in a group.

Part of Chris's reluctance to share was caused by a broken confidence years ago. Commit to one another that whatever is shared here, stays here. Confidentiality is foundational to building a caring community.

Beginning ▼▼▼▼▼▼▼▼▼▼▼▼▼▼▼▼▼▼ 15 minutes

❶ *Read aloud the following introduction to sharing questions. Once you're finished reading, go around the room allowing each person to answer the first question before moving to the next one. You may choose to answer first each time.*

Most of us have some memories (often fond ones) of some aspect of our childhood. Where we spent our early years, where we went for comfort, and when and if the idea of God was a part of our lives are issues that affect who we are today. A new group spends a lot of time telling these stories because the more we know about each other, the better we will understand how to participate with God in each other's lives. We earn one another's trust gradually by offering our stories and listening to the stories of others.

If you are uncomfortable answering these questions, feel free to say, "I pass," and the group will go on to the next person.

1. Where were you living at age ten? How many brothers and sisters lived in your household?

2. a. When you were a child, what was one thing you liked to do on your own?

   b. What was one thing you liked to do with a group?

3. To where or whom did you turn for comfort?

4. Who was God to you when you were a child?
   ❑ a policeman who was waiting for me to make a mistake
   ❑ someone I thought about a lot
   ❑ someone I didn't think about much
   ❑ like a grandfather, kind and loving
   ❑ other:

The Text ▼▼▼▼▼▼▼▼▼▼▼▼▼▼▼▼▼▼▼▼ 5 minutes

Jesus began his ministry by gathering a small group of followers. Some knew each other well; they were brothers. Others were strangers. They came from a variety of backgrounds, professions, and political views. But they had one thing in common: they all wanted to know Jesus. In this way they resembled our small group today. As you read and listen to this passage, imagine yourself as Andrew or James, called to join Jesus' group.

❶ *Ask for a volunteer to read the text aloud. You may also read some or all of the reference notes on page 17.*

After John was arrested, Jesus went to Galilee preaching **the Message of God**: "Time's up! **God's kingdom** is here. **Change your life** and believe the Message."

Passing along the beach of Lake Galilee, he saw **Simon** and his brother **Andrew** net-fishing. Fishing was their regular work. Jesus said to them, "Come with me. I'll make a new kind of fisherman out of you. I'll show you how to catch men and women instead of perch and bass." They didn't ask questions. They dropped their nets and followed.

A dozen yards or so down the beach, he saw the brothers **James and John**, Zebedee's sons. They were in the boat, mending their fishnets. Right off, he made the same offer. Immediately, they left their father Zebedee, the boat, the hired hands, and followed. . . .

Strolling along, he saw **Levi**, son of Alphaeus, at his work **collecting taxes**. Jesus said, "Come along with me." He came.

(Mark 1:14-20, 2:14, MSG)

▼▼▼▼▼▼▼▼ ▼ ▼ ▼ ▼ ▼ ▼ ▼ ▼ ▼▼ ▼▼
Understanding the Text   10 minutes

5. How did Jesus recruit these five people into his group?

6. What did he recruit them to do?

7. Read the reference note on page 17 about God's kingdom. Why was it radical for Jesus to announce, "God's kingdom is here"?

8. How do you think joining Jesus' group changed the lives of these men?

Applying the Text ▼ ▼ ▼ ▼ ▼ ▼ ▼ ▼ ▼ ▼ ▼ ▼ ▼ ▼ ▼ ▼ 20 minutes

9. What would have been going through your mind if you were in James' shoes that night, after a day with Jesus and these other guys?

   ❏ This is great!
   ❏ This is okay, but I need to get back to work.
   ❏ Finally—something more important to do than fishing!
   ❏ What have I done?!
   ❏ I'm a bit out of my comfort zone, but there's something about this Jesus that fascinates me.
   ❏ Jesus I like, but the rest of these guys—I dunno.
   ❏ My father is going to kill me.
   ❏ Other:

10. What drew you to this small group?

    ❏ I want to get to know some other people who want to follow Jesus.
    ❏ Somebody said a small group could help me grow spiritually.
    ❏ I wasn't drawn; I was dragged here by:
    ❏ Other:

11. In what ways do you think our small group's purpose should be like the purpose of Jesus' group? In what ways do you think it should be different?

12. a. Read the section, "Building Community," in the Introduction on pages 5–6. Which aspects of this section are most attractive to you?

  b. Do you have any questions or concerns about this statement? Explain.

Assignment ▼▼▼▼▼▼▼▼▼▼▼▼▼▼▼▼▼▼ 5 minutes

► Before you leave, pass around your books and have everyone sign the group phone list on page 79.

► (*Optional*) Ask if someone would volunteer to bring a simple snack for the next meeting.

► Notice the empty chair in the room where you are meeting. It represents a safe place where you can invite a friend, coworker, or family member to join next time. During the week, think about whom you might invite to join the next meeting.

Prayer ▼▼▼▼▼▼▼▼▼▼▼▼▼▼▼▼▼▼ 5 minutes

Stand in a circle. Hold hands if you are comfortable doing so. Let each person pray aloud, beginning with the leader. If you like, simply finish this prayer: "Dear God, thanks for. . . ." If you would rather pray silently, please say "Amen" aloud to let the other people know you are finished.

▼ ▼ ▼ ▼ ▼ ▼ ▼ ▼ ▼ ▼ ▼ ▼ ▼ ▼ ▼ ▼ ▼ ▼ ▼
Reference Notes

Setting: The first major section of Mark's gospel includes a summary statement of Jesus' message as well as the calling of his first disciples. John the Baptist had just been arrested and jailed. John had preached that God's kingdom and chosen King (the Messiah) were coming soon; Jesus picked up where John left off.

The Message of God: "Message" is a translation of the Greek word *euangelion,* which means "good message" or "good news"; and it also gives us words like "evangelist." Jesus' message was God's good news for men and women.

God's kingdom: God's present and ongoing reign; God's sovereign activity of ruling over his realm. The Old Testament had predicted that God's kingdom would be a realm of peace, abundance, and justice and would be ushered in by a King, the Messiah. By proclaiming that God's kingdom had arrived, Jesus was also implying that God's King had arrived. John the Baptist had urged people to prepare for the coming King; Jesus announced that the time of preparation was over.

Change your life: Those who wanted to follow Jesus had to change or repent—turn away from their sinful lifestyle of disregarding God in day-to-day decisions and events. Believers of the Message were those who committed themselves wholeheartedly to that Message and its messenger: Jesus.

Simon, Andrew, James and John: Unlike most rabbis of the day, who were sought out by their pupils and apprentices, Jesus did not wait for these two pairs of brothers to seek him. Jesus gave Simon the nickname, "Peter," which meant "little rock." James and John he called "Sons of Thunder." Simon Peter and Andrew had been followers of John the Baptist (John 1:35–42). James and John came from a comparatively prosperous fishing family that could afford to hire helpers.

Levi . . . collecting taxes: Levi also went by the name Matthew (Matthew 9:9–13). Jews hated tax collectors because they were fellow Jews who collaborated with the oppressive Roman invaders. Taxes were exorbitantly high, and tax collectors made their living through extortion of those they taxed. One can hardly imagine someone whom the fishermen would want less as part of their group.

Believing for Each Other

❶ *Arrive early enough to speak with the host(s) and to pray with them. Welcome everyone as they arrive. It always helps to have a pot of coffee on. People generally loosen up and talk more freely if they have something warm in their hand! Start on time.*

▼ ▼
Overview   5 minutes

❶ *Welcome group members and remind them you are glad they returned. Tell them you are excited to be a part of this group. Then take thirty seconds and tell them what to expect during the meeting.*

I remember when I hurt my back and was laid up for weeks. When I began to recover, I felt the pressure of having fallen behind in the repair and upkeep of our home, but my back was so tender that I couldn't even wheel the garbage cans out to the street for collection. Pretty soon my pride felt as bruised as my back.

My wife suggested I ask for help from others in our small group. At first I resisted. But the longer I waited, the more my back ached, which broke down my reluctance to let her make the call. When she sent out an SOS on my behalf, help came flooding in! One man in the group said they were wondering what they could do to help me, but it appeared to them that we had everything covered. I had to endure a lot of pain before I could ask others to help me, but I now greatly value the support of my fellow group members.

In this session we will discuss this issue. We will continue to get to know each other by telling more about ourselves. Next, we'll compare the biblical story of Jesus and the paraplegic to our own stories, and explore our need for a supportive group of friends who can help us listen and act upon what God asks of us. We'll have an optional time of worship early in our meeting, and time to share prayer requests at the end.

❶ *At this point, share any group business that needs to be covered. Ask if anyone has any announcements that need to be made. Suggest that in the future, you would like to know about any announcements before the meeting begins.*

▼ ▼ ▼ ▼ ▼ ▼ ▼ ▼ ▼ ▼ ▼ ▼ ▼ ▼ ▼ ▼ ▼ ▼ ▼
Assignment Debriefing   5 minutes

Last week you talked briefly about the empty chair. Did anyone think about a person in your circle of influence who would benefit from being in your group? Remember, each of you has five circles of influence (page 73):

- ▶ Family—parents, children, siblings, cousins, etc.
- ▶ Friends—those you enjoy spending time with (entertainment, study, etc.)
- ▶ Coworkers—peers, bosses, those you supervise, or people you go to school with
- ▶ Neighbors—people who live around you
- ▶ Fun—people with whom you share hobbies, sports, etc.

If you have thought of a person, do you need help inviting him or her? Or, can you share how you extended an invitation?

Beginning 20 minutes

1. What three key words would you choose to describe yourself, without mentioning anything about what you do for a living? For example, think of:

   ❒ Qualities (smart, sensitive, energetic)
   ❒ Values (fun-loving, thrifty, dependable)
   ❒ Talents and pleasures (singer, chef, golfer)

2. When do you feel most accepted?

   ❒ When I am with my family
   ❒ When I am with my friends
   ❒ When someone asks me to do something with them
   ❒ When someone gives me a compliment
   ❒ Other:

3. Answer one of the following:

   a. What was the best compliment you have received lately? How did it make you feel?

   b. Which of God's qualities attracts you to him? Why?

The Text 5 minutes

Everywhere Jesus went, he attracted large crowds of people. Many wanted to see him, to hear what he had to say. Some came to him with ailments that seemed to have no cure. He had compassion on them and took time for each one. As we look at a story about the courage of a small group of friends, consider what it might have been like to be one of the paralytic's friends.

❶ *Ask for a volunteer to read the text aloud. You may also read some or all of the reference notes on page 26.*

After a few days, Jesus returned to **Capernaum**, and word got around that he was back home. A crowd gathered, jamming the entrance so no one could get in or out. He was teaching the Word. They brought a **paraplegic** to him, carried by four men. When they weren't able to get in because of the crowd, they removed **part of the roof** and lowered the paraplegic on his stretcher. **Impressed** by their bold belief, Jesus said to the paraplegic, "**Son**, I forgive **your sins**."
  Some religious scholars sitting there started whispering among themselves, "He can't talk that way! That's blasphemy! God and only God can forgive sins."
  Jesus knew right away what they were thinking, and said, "Why are you so skeptical? Which is simpler: to say to the paraplegic, 'I forgive your sins,' or say, 'Get up, take your stretcher, and start walking'? Well, just so it's clear that I'm the Son of Man and authorized to do either, or both . . . " (he looked now at the paraplegic), "**Get up. Pick up your stretcher and go home.**" And the man did it—got up, grabbed his stretcher, and walked out, with everyone there watching him. They rubbed their eyes, incredulous—and then praised God, saying, "We've never seen anything like this!"

(Mark 2:1-12, MSG)

▼ ▼ ▼ ▼ ▼ ▼ ▼ ▼   ▼   ▼   ▼ ▼   ▼   ▼   ▼   ▼ ▼ ▼
Understanding the Text   10 minutes

  4. How did the paraplegic's friends get Jesus' attention?

  5. What motivated Jesus to heal this man?

6. Why do you think Jesus talked about forgiving this man's sins before Jesus healed him?

Applying the Text
20 minutes

7. What connection is there between a person's faith and God's activity on their behalf? What about the faith of a person's friends?

8. What would have been your response if you had been in this group, and someone had suggested that you dig a hole in the roof?

   ❑ You're crazy!
   ❑ You go ahead, I'll watch from over here.
   ❑ That's a bad idea, let's look for a better solution.
   ❑ Whatever it takes!
   ❑ Other:

9. What aspects of our society make it hard for us to depend on other people?

10. When do you need help from friends?

    ❑ Not often. I get along all right by myself.
    ❑ Only when I am in way over my head.
    ❑ Occasionally when I am working on:
    ❑ Once a year at tax time!
    ❑ I rarely need help, but I'm glad there are a few others I can call on.
    ❑ Constantly, because:
    ❑ Other:

11. Is Jesus asking you to express your faith in him? Is it to trust him for salvation? To deepen your trust and dependence upon him? Explain.

12. In what particular area of your life would you like to ask Jesus to move? Do you need healing? forgiveness? Can you share one of these needs with the group?

Prayer   5 minutes

Close this meeting with an opportunity for everyone to share a personal prayer request and to be prayed for. Here are some guidelines.

Use the ABCs of group prayer:

About yourself. Requests ought to be limited to you and your own family of origin or immediate relationships. This is not the time to pray for distant relatives, casual friends, or global issues. These areas would probably be better addressed in an organized prayer meeting or some other venue.

Brief. You really do not need to go into all the history and details. Try to be concise and specific.

Counseling not permitted. This is a time for prayer, not extensive counseling. Feel free to share briefly how you have been encouraged by the Word, or how God has cared for you during a similar time in your life, but keep the focus on prayer and the expressed need of the individual.

Make a covenant of confidentiality. Whatever is shared here, stays here. It is essential that each and every member of the group is convinced that this group is a safe place for them.

Learn to treat prayer as a natural activity for Christians. Many people have not had a model of conversational prayer—that is, prayer in a normal, conversational style. The effectiveness of a prayer style is really not the issue; your growing confidence is. Seek to grow more comfortable with each other, more willing to share your hearts' concerns with God your Father and with the group as your witness. As you grow together, religious language or traditions may become less important as you learn how to pray to a God who understands you when you speak in everyday language.

❶ *Remember, the leader leads! You will set the tone, the level of transparency and vulnerability in prayer. Try to establish a balance between too little and too much. It is important for your group members to know you need prayer. Many people think leaders in the church are above sin and temptation. Start with yourself, and many others will follow your lead.*

▼▼▼▼▼▼▼▼▼▼▼▼▼▼▼▼▼▼▼▼
Assignment   5 minutes

Ask if someone would volunteer to bring a simple snack for the next meeting. Remember the empty chair in your meeting room. It represents a safe place where you can invite a friend, coworker, or family member to join next week. If you have not thought of a person, would you make this a matter of prayer this week? Also, try to be aware of those around you who might need a helping hand.

▼▼▼▼▼▼▼▼▼▼▼▼▼▼▼▼▼▼▼▼
Reference Notes

Setting: This event occurred early in Jesus' ministry. As a result, his enemies began to think that Jesus might be dangerous. He claimed authority to forgive sin, which only God could claim.

Capernaum: A small, mostly Jewish town in the north of Roman-controlled Palestine. Jesus made it his home base for his northern ministry, since he grew up just a few miles away.

Paraplegic: The man was at least partially paralyzed.

Part of the roof: Jesus was not teaching in a synagogue, but in a home. Like many Palestine houses in this period, there was a stairway going up to the roof which was made of a composite of clay, grass, clay tiles, and laths. Digging through the roof would have made a real mess damaging the roof and causing quite a disturbance.

Impressed: Jesus was impressed, rather than annoyed, by this mess and interruption.

Son: A term of affection.

Your sins: In that culture, disease and death were viewed as the consequences of a person's sinful condition. The Old Testament says that disease and death are the results of human sinfulness. Sometimes a disease is the result of the sick person's sin; at other times it results from the corrupt state of humanity and the world in general.

Get up: A test of faith.

Pick up your stretcher and go home: A demand for obedience.

Many Parts Working Together

Overview ▼▼▼▼▼▼▼▼▼▼▼▼▼▼▼▼▼▼▼▼ 5 minutes

❶ *Begin on time, and briefly outline the agenda for the meeting.*

As we spend time together, our similarities and differences become more and more apparent. Some of us are more verbal, some more reserved. Some have had varied and exciting experiences; others have lived away from the "fast lane." All of us are important because the group is enriched with each of our personalities. All of our experiences have affected who we are and help to determine how much we interact with others around us.

I was brought up in an era when there was still much value placed on being a "self-made man," holding true to the pioneer spirit that helped to create our country. My father believed in it as well. Consequently, getting my worth from hard work and trying to figure things out myself became my way of life. But the longer I walk as a follower of Jesus, the more I realize that it is what he says about me that is important. He has invited me to become a part of the whole, and in many ways to pour my life into the mix that paints the big picture.

In this session we will examine the concept of being one among many and what this means to us as individuals. We will look at the similarities between some of the issues the church of Corinth faced and the issues we face today. As before, we'll also tell more of our stories, take a few minutes to worship God through a psalm, and pray for each other at the end of our meeting.

Finally, we will add a Personal Learning Diary section in this and our remaining sessions. It will be a time for you to record thoughts, ideas, feelings, and personal prayers, that are prompted by the meeting.

Assignment Debriefing 5 minutes

1. Does anyone want to praise God for something he has done this week, an answer to a prayer from our last meeting, or something new about your faith you have discovered? (Please keep prayer requests until later in the meeting.)

Beginning 20 minutes

2. If the people who know you best were asked, would they say you are usually predictable or unpredictable? Why? Do you tend to follow a set routine, or do you often do the same things differently?

3. Which of these traits do you value most in a friend? Why?

The Text 5 minutes

There is so much talk about diversity today. We think it is some new concept advanced by those who want us all to be "politically correct." According to the apostle Paul's letter to the believers in Corinth, it has been a biblically correct concept for at least 2,000 years!

I spent a lot of time during my high school and college years trying to be different so I could make a statement about my individuality. I wore wild clothing, shoes, hair styles, and hair lengths in order to be cool. Looking back on those years, with much fondness and some embarrassment, I can see that my yearning for individuality was mostly a cry for someone to say, "You are acceptable to me, regardless of how you look, what you've done, or where you've been." Jesus reminds me that this is exactly how he looks upon me, and you.

❶ *Ask for a volunteer to read the text aloud. You may also read some or all of the reference notes on page 33.*

You can easily enough see how . . . [*the division of gifts among the group*] works by looking no further than your own body. Your body has many parts—limbs, organs, cells—but no matter how many parts you can name, you're still one body. It's exactly the same with Christ. By means of his one Spirit, we all said goodbye to our partial and piecemeal lives. We each used to independently call our own shots, but then we entered into a large and integrated life in which *he* has the final say in everything. (This is what we proclaimed in word and action when we were baptized.) Each of us is now a part of his resurrection body, refreshed and sustained at one fountain—his Spirit—where we all come to drink. The old labels we once used to identify ourselves—labels like **Jew or Greek, slave or free**—are no longer useful. We need something larger, more comprehensive.

I want you to think about how all this makes you more significant, not less. A body isn't just a single part blown up into something huge. It's all the different-but-similar parts arranged and functioning together. If Foot said, "I'm not elegant like Hand, embellished with rings; I guess I don't belong to this body," would that make it so? If Ear said, "I'm not beautiful like Eye, limpid and expressive; I don't deserve a place on the head," would you want to remove it from the body? If the body was all eye, how could it hear? If all ear, how could it smell? As it is, we see that God has carefully placed each part of the body right where he wanted it.

(1 Corinthians 12:12-20, MSG)

Understanding the Text ▼▼▼▼▼▼▼▼▼ 10 minutes

4. Why do you think Paul wants us to see the church as a human body?

5. What do you think happens to a small group of God's people if they don't get the idea that everyone is necessary to the group and equal in importance?

6. Using the analogy of the body, which part do you feel best describes your work/position/function among God's people?

   ❏ Ear—I am a good listener.
   ❏ Eye—I look for good things in others.
   ❏ Mouth—I try to be encouraging to others.
   ❏ Nose—I am drawn to:
   ❏ Feet—I deliver good news to others.
   ❏ Hands—I like to pray, or I like to:
   ❏ Other:

Applying the Text ▼▼▼▼▼▼▼▼▼▼ 20 minutes

7. a. What obstacles do you think could prevent your group from functioning effectively as a body?

b. How can you avoid or overcome those obstacles?

8. Can you think of instances where churches in your area were able to work together? If so, name one. If not, why do you suppose that's the case?

9. Using the body as a picture of our need to be unified and working toward the same goal, what part (or person) do you need to work better with?

▼ ▼ ▼ ▼ ▼ ▼ ▼ ▼ ▼ ▼ ▼ ▼ ▼ ▼ ▼ ▼ ▼ ▼ ▼ ▼ ▼
Prayer   10 minutes

❶ *Ask if anyone would like prayer. If the group is small, it may be good to keep the whole group together. If it is larger, you may want to break up the group into groups of two or three to pray. Tell them where in the house to go (check this out with the host ahead of time). Let everyone know that you will give them notice after 10 minutes. (You may extend the prayer time.) Keep prayer requests limited to yourself, spouse, children, etc. Do not counsel. It is appropriate to share your experience if it is directly related, but most often it is better to listen attentively and then to pray. Finally, remember the covenant of confidentiality. Whatever is shared here, stays here. It is essential that every member of the group is convinced that this group is a safe place for them.*

❶ *Bring the group back together. Do a quick review of what you learned and discussed together tonight.*

31

Personal Learning Diary   5 minutes

Take a few moments at the end of the group time to be quiet
and reflect. Record your answers, thoughts, feelings, and ideas
about the following: What did I learn, see, experience tonight?
Did I have an "aha" moment?

Assignment   5 minutes

► As each person in your group is a part of the body, so
  also this group is a part of two larger bodies: your
  church and the Body of Christ. During the coming
  week, meditate on this question: "What does this mean
  to our group and to me personally?"

► Who will volunteer to bring a simple snack for the next
  meeting?

► Remember that the empty chair in the room represents
  a safe place where you can invite a friend, coworker, or
  family member to join next week.

▼▼▼▼▼▼▼▼▼▼▼▼▼▼▼▼▼▼▼▼▼
Reference Notes

Setting: The apostle Paul founded the church in Corinth, Greece. The church was comprised of several home groups not much larger than yours. About three years after Paul left Corinth, word came back to him about problems in the groups:

> ► Factions were ripping the church apart (chapters 1–4).
> ► Sexual immorality was contaminating the church members (chapters 5–6).
> ► They were dragging one another into civil court, trying to resolve their conflicts (chapter 6).
> ► They argued over the relative merits of singleness and marriage (chapter 7).
> ► They fought about whether it was proper to eat meat sold at pagan temples (chapters 8–10).
> ► They abused the Lord's Supper (chapter 11).
> ► They were divided over whose contributions to the group were most important (chapters 11–14).
> ► They allowed false teachings about the resurrection (chapter 15).

Paul wrote 1 Corinthians to address those problems. Competitiveness lay at the core of them all.

Jew or Greek, slave or free: Corinthian society tended to divide along ethnic and class divisions like these. Wealth was another major opportunity for discrimination.

Planning Our Future

❶ *Since you will work on a group covenant in this session, you should find out ahead of time your pastor's or church's policy concerning the various tenets of the covenant outline below.*

Overview ▼▼▼▼▼▼▼▼▼▼▼▼▼▼▼▼▼▼ 5 minutes

A while back, when the Department of Transportation mandated that all guardrails be built into the ground or finished with a curled end, the state of Florida set out to comply. A peculiarity developed in the Florida Keys (a series of small islands connected with bridges or built-up connecting roads). For years there had not been any incidents of cars driving off the roads into the water, but in the few weeks when the guardrails were down for replacement, many drivers lost control and drove their vehicles into the ocean! Without proper guidelines or boundaries, we can quickly lose our sense of direction and purpose.

Several years ago, my wife and I joined a group with four other couples in our church. We met for brunch to discuss the guidelines for our group. We agreed that leadership would rotate—when a couple hosted the group, they would also lead it. Our group covenant included two other helpful clauses: (1) I would not become the default leader, so I could be a regular member of the group and the leader every fifth time; and (2) We would not discuss the decisions or the character of other pastors and leaders of the church.

One Sunday evening when I was teaching elsewhere, the

group met. Over coffee, someone mentioned a statement made during the sermon earlier that day. The conversation moved quickly to the character and personality of the preaching pastor. Within a few moments, one of the group members pulled a copy of the group covenant out and reminded the group that it was off course. End of discussion. The group covenant had reminded us of prior healthy decisions, and pointed us back to the reason for meeting.

This illustrates the value of a group covenant. We have already agreed on one element of a covenant: the rule of confidentiality. In this session we will discuss other possible ground rules for the group and agree on the commitments we want to make. We will also examine a passage from Paul's second letter to the church at Corinth that describes the "focused center" around which Paul organized his groups. Because the discussion of our covenant will take considerable time, we will not take time to worship at the beginning of this meeting, but we will pray for each other at the end.

Assignment Debriefing   5 minutes

1. Does anyone have any further thoughts about what it means for you to be part of the Body of Christ? (Please keep prayer requests until later in the meeting.)

Beginning   30 minutes

2. What is the best imaginable plan you could make for your life in the next 5 years? How do you think you would handle it, if it were to happen?

❶ *Take a moment to pray for God's guidance as you define your group covenant.*

Small-Group Covenant or Ground Rules

A covenant is a set of ground rules that help to establish boundaries and encourage a safe-place mentality. Every small group should have a covenant that has been discussed and developed by the members. With a clear, written covenant, you have a road map to help you achieve the group's goals. Without clearly defined goals, a group can become aimless, introspective, and unhealthy. A copy of the covenant can be given to any new attendees to help them understand who you are and where the group is going. Feel free to customize the covenant, using the outline below as a basis for discussion and brainstorming. If you run short of time, go on to the Bible study and return to the covenant in your next meeting.

You'll notice that some of the statements are about "we" and "us," while others are about "I" and "me." Sometimes it helps to state commitments not just for "us" (what I expect you to do), but also for "me" (what I am committing to do for you).

Ground rules vary, but the following are elements to consider. On item 1, see the comments under "Establishing the Purpose of Your Group" in the leader's appendix, page 70.

1. The reason our group exists is:

2. Our specific group goals include:

3. We meet ____ time(s) a month, and this covenant will be in effect for ____ weeks/months. At the end of the covenant period, we will evaluate our progress and growth.

4. We will meet on _____ (day of week), from _____ till _____ (meeting time).

5. Our meetings will be held at _____ (location).

6. Our group will be (choose one):

   ▶ open (continually open to new members)
   ▶ closed (not open after the third meeting)
   ▶ a combination (open during certain times, such as when we begin a new study guide, at the beginning of a new year, or four times a year)

7. We agree to the following group disciplines (choose one or more):

   ▶ Attendance—We will be here whenever possible. This group will be a priority.
   ▶ Ownership—We agree to share responsibility for the group and our goals.
   ▶ Confidentiality—We agree to keep here whatever is shared here.
   ▶ Accountability—We give each other permission to hold us accountable for the goals we set.
   ▶ Accessibility—We give one another permission to call at any hour when there is a need.

8. Our plan for service and outreach (to the church, our neighborhood, our community, etc.) needs to be discussed and developed. (See additional ideas and information in session 6.)

9. Other possible ground rules:

   ▶ Food and snacks (Who's responsible for bringing what?)
   ▶ Child care
   ▶ Group leadership (Will there be a single leader with an apprentice, or rotating leadership?)
   ▶ A plan for growth and eventual multiplication into two groups
   ▶ Fun and recreation (To round out a group and keep it vibrant, it's advisable to plan occasional fun nights and recreational outings. Many have found it useful to add a fun time every six to eight meetings.)

The Text ▼▼▼▼▼▼▼▼▼▼▼▼▼▼▼▼▼▼▼▼▼▼ 5 minutes

Israel's covenants with God and each other always grew from a focused center: God's acts of compassion that bound the people to him. In the same way, our covenants with each other must grow from the focused center of what God has done for us. In this passage from Paul's second letter to Corinth, Paul describes our mission that emerges from this focused center.

❶ *Ask for a volunteer to read the text aloud. You may also read some or all of the reference notes on page 43.*

Our firm decision is to work from this focused center: One man died for everyone. That puts everyone in the same boat. He included everyone in his death so that everyone could also be included in his life, a resurrection life, a far better life than people ever lived on their own.

Because of this decision we don't evaluate people by what they have or how they look. **We looked at the Messiah that way once** and got it all wrong, as you know. We certainly don't look at him that way anymore. Now we look inside, and what we see is that anyone united with the Messiah gets a fresh start, is created new. **The old life is gone**; a new life burgeons! Look at it! All this comes from the God who settled the relationship between us and him, and then called us to settle our relationships with each other. God put the world square with himself through the Messiah, giving the world a fresh start by offering forgiveness of sins. God has given us the task of telling everyone what he is doing. We're **Christ's representatives.** God uses us to persuade men and women to drop their differences and enter into God's work of making things right between them. We're speaking for Christ himself now: Become friends with God; he's already a friend with you.

(2 Corinthians 5:14–20, MSG)

3. What do you think it means to be "created new"?

    ❐ To look different
    ❐ To have different friends
    ❐ To feel different
    ❐ To look at life differently
    ❐ To have new values
    ❐ To have new options
    ❐ Other:

4. Do you know someone whose life has changed substantially because of new faith in Christ? How would you describe that person's change?

5. What is our job on earth, according to Paul?

6. How does it feel to think of yourself as Christ's official representative?

    ❐ I'm impressed.
    ❐ I'm intimidated.
    ❐ I'm proud.
    ❐ I'm excited.
    ❐ I feel inadequate.
    ❐ I feel:

7. Paul tells the Corinthians, who are already believers, to "become friends with God." Why would he say this to believers?

Applying the Text

God often uses us to persuade others to drop their differences. Though reconciliation is difficult to apply, the results can be wonderful.

A few years ago I attended a leader training event where the speaker talked a great deal about reconciliation. It became apparent to me that I needed to pursue reconciliation with my father. We had an amicable relationship, but there were years of "stuff" that had not been dealt with between us. Most of the "stuff" was due to my rebellion and hard-headed approach to life in my earlier years. Wow! I thought. How do I begin to fix fifteen years of bruised feelings and a broken relationship? It was an overwhelming task. Then it dawned on me: I couldn't fix it, but Jesus could! I asked for extra grace to begin and wrote my Dad a letter, saying that I would like to meet with him to begin the process.

It took me over a week to actually drop the letter in the mail. Within a few days my father called me, and we set a time for my mother and him to come and visit. When the time came for their visit, I was almost frozen with fear. If Jesus through the Holy Spirit didn't come through, things would surely get worse and. . . .

They arrived. It went well. The Holy Spirit had been preparing my father's heart as well, and we have been growing deeper in our friendship and our renewed relationship as father and son. It is surely worth the price!

8. Assuming that becoming friends with God is an ongoing process, in what way(s) do you need to become friends with God?

9. Can you think of anyone with whom you have a broken relationship that you need to restore? What can you do?

▼▼▼ ▼ ▼ ▼ ▼ ▼ ▼ ▼ ▼ ▼ ▼ ▼ ▼ ▼ ▼ ▼ ▼ ▼ ▼
Prayer   5 minutes

❶ *Ask a question: "If Jesus were to come and take part in our group, what would you ask him to reconcile in your life?" Again allow opportunity for the members to share personal issues for which they would like to receive prayer. Determine whether the group should stay together as a whole or break into sub-groups of three or four.*

Remember the basic parameters and boundaries for sharing and praying for one another.

▼ ▼ ▼ ▼ ▼ ▼ ▼ ▼ ▼ ▼ ▼ ▼ ▼ ▼ ▼ ▼ ▼ ▼ ▼
Personal Learning Diary   5 minutes

► What did I learn? experience? feel? How does this affect my understanding of my relationship with God? My responsibility as Christ's representative?

► *(Optional)* In my current position and situation I can use this understanding to:

► I plan on developing my skills in my current position and situation by:

Assignment

▼ ▼ ▼ ▼ ▼ ▼ ▼ ▼ ▼ ▼ ▼ ▼ ▼ ▼ ▼ ▼ ▼ ▼ ▼

If you were unable to complete the work on your group covenant, take some time this week to consider the other components and write down your ideas in the margins. You will take some time at the beginning of the next session to discuss the covenant and commit to your set of ground rules.

Reference Notes

▼ ▼ ▼ ▼ ▼ ▼ ▼ ▼ ▼ ▼ ▼ ▼ ▼ ▼ ▼ ▼ ▼ ▼ ▼

Setting: Throughout 2 Corinthians, Paul defends his ministry as a messenger of God's new covenant with people. This passage is Paul's central definition of his ministry.

We looked at the Messiah that way once: Before encountering the risen Christ personally, Paul battled zealously to execute everyone who believed in Jesus as heretics. It was inconceivable to Paul that God's chosen King, the Messiah, could have died a contemptible death on a cross. The Messiah had to be someone powerful and successful, according to Paul's assumptions. Paul had been well-trained in a particular reading of the Old Testament that ruled out the possibility of a crucified Savior.

The old life is gone: This does not mean that our memories and habits are erased when we trust in Christ, but rather that we have started a new life that draws its strength from God's Spirit. It generally takes some time for this new life to permeate our thought patterns and habits.

Christ's representatives: The term means "ambassador," one who carries the full authority of the head of state. We carry Christ's full authority to make peace between God and other people.

43

Becoming a Caring Community

Overview 5–15 minutes

Building community is an adventure. Like any adventure, it takes careful planning, communication, and sometimes perseverance. Building a caring community also requires mutual care and encouragement to feed the participants in this adventure. When I lead seminars on small groups, I often ask, "How many of you have received too much encouragement lately? How about just enough encouragement?" These questions are usually met by nervous laughter. Why is that? Maybe because we often feel we are treated like one of the faceless masses. Perhaps it is because our society is becoming insulated; it's considered unsafe or inconvenient to go out of one's way to assist strangers. Many pressures work against open, encouraging, and caring relationships. Maybe this is the time for the Church to shine!

In this session we will first finish our discussion of a covenant, if necessary. Then we'll worship, and afterward we'll explore how to encourage, accept, and love one another. We will examine what Paul told the church in Rome and discuss how his words apply to us. At the close of our meeting, we'll pray together and take some time for our Personal Learning Diaries, and we'll begin to pray for each other outside the group.

▼▼▼▼▼▼▼▼▼ ▼ ▼ ▼ ▼ ▼ ▼ ▼▼▼ ▼
Assignment Debriefing   5 minutes

1. Does anyone want to praise God for something he has done
   this week, an answer to a prayer from our last meeting, or
   something new about your faith you have discovered?
   (Please keep prayer requests until later in the meeting.)

   ❶ *Pass out copies of your group covenant or ground rules.*
   Use this time to review what you decided as a group at your
   last meeting. If you need additional time this week to finish
   your work, invite the group members to share their ideas from
   last session's assignment.

▼ ▼ ▼ ▼ ▼ ▼ ▼ ▼ ▼ ▼ ▼ ▼ ▼ ▼ ▼ ▼ ▼ ▼ ▼
Beginning   20 minutes

2. What has been one of the best compliments you have
   received as an adult?

3. Can you remember a special compliment you received as a
   child? How did it affect your life?

   ❶ *Pass out slips of paper two to three inches long and one*
   inch wide. Ask each person to write down his or her name,
   address, and phone number (if you feel everyone in the group
   is comfortable with exchanging this information). Pass around
   a jar and ask each person to fold his slip of paper and deposit it
   in the jar. Put this aside until later.

▼ ▼ ▼ ▼ ▼ ▼ ▼ ▼ ▼ ▼ ▼ ▼ ▼ ▼ ▼ ▼ ▼ ▼ ▼ ▼
The Text   5 minutes

A while ago when I was leading a group, a new person came but chose to remain quiet through most of the meeting. After listening to the rest of us share a little about ourselves and discuss the Scripture we were studying, she finally broke in. Her statement shocked and challenged us. She said, "I don't have a clue what you are talking about, but I sense something in this group I have never sensed before. What is going on here?" It was both a bewildering and wonderful inquiry. A couple of the group members tried to shift the subject because they felt uncomfortable with her admission. I asked everyone to set aside our agenda for a few moments so we could address our guest's questions. We were so caught in our agenda, and in our pursuit of our growth and relationships, that we almost missed the gift God had sent us in this woman who was seeking! We took time to share with her the gospel of Jesus and gave her an invitation to become a fellow pilgrim. She grew week by week and a few months later proclaimed her decision to follow Christ and become his disciple. What a party we had that night!

Being accepted or acceptable is something many of us struggle with in subtle ways. Learning to accept others can set us free from this problem. In this passage from Paul's letter to the church in Rome, Paul describes how to accept, encourage, and love each other.

❶ *Ask for a volunteer to read the text aloud. You may also read some or all of the reference notes on page 51.*

Those of us who are **strong** and able in the faith need to step in and lend a hand to those who falter, and not just do what is most convenient for us. Strength is for service, not status. Each one of us needs to look after the good of the people around us, asking ourselves, "How can I help?"

That's exactly what Jesus did. He didn't make it easy for himself by avoiding people's troubles, but waded right in and helped out. "I took on the troubles of the troubled," is the way the Scripture puts it. Even if it was written in Scripture long ago, you can be sure it's written for *us*. God wants the combination of his steady, constant calling and warm, personal counsel in Scripture to come to characterize *us*, keeping us alert for whatever he will do next. May our dependably steady and warmly personal God develop maturity in you so that you get along with each other as well as Jesus gets along with us all. Then we'll be a choir—not our voices only, but our very lives singing in harmony in a stunning anthem to the God and Father of our Master Jesus!

So reach out and **welcome one another to God's glory**. Jesus did it; now *you* do it!

(Romans 15:1–7, MSG)

Understanding the Text   20 minutes

4. Who do you think are "those of us who are strong"?

5. Who are "those who falter"?

6. What do you think Paul means when he says, "Each one of us needs to look after the good of the people around us"?

   ❏ be nice to them
   ❏ mow their grass
   ❏ bake them some cookies
   ❏ pray for them
   ❏ do something their way instead of our way
   ❏ take time to listen to them
   ❏ other:

7. What purposes for the Scriptures does Paul describe in this passage?

8. What does God want to develop in us, and why is that important?

Applying the Text   20 minutes

9. How can we "look after the good of the people around us," in particular, in our group? How can I help you? How can you help me?

10. What can you do this week to get along better with those you come in contact with?

Prayer   5 minutes

❶ *You may want to direct the prayer time by suggesting that requests focus on the following: "Whom do I need to be more accepting of?" or "I need encouragement in the following area . . . ."*

Assignment ▼▼▼▼▼▼▼▼▼▼▼▼▼▼▼▼▼▼ 10 minutes

❶ *Pass around the jar and ask each person to draw out a name. Everyone should immediately open and read the name silently to ensure she did not select her own. Then challenge the group to practice what they learned from Romans.*

Please commit to pray this week for the person whose name you drew. If you feel so motivated, you might also call that person or drop him a note to encourage him in some way.

Personal Learning Diary ▼▼▼▼▼▼▼▼▼▼▼▼▼▼▼ 5 minutes

What did I learn, experience, or feel in this session?

Reference Notes ▼▼▼▼▼▼▼▼▼▼▼▼▼▼▼

Setting: The house-churches in Rome to whom Paul wrote included both Jews and Gentiles. Jews and Gentiles had a very poor history of getting along with each other. The Jews thought Gentiles were disgusting because they ate foods which were forbidden in the Old Testament, buried their dead relatives on the family property (Jewish law forbade such close contact with the dead), and were uncircumcised. The Gentiles thought circumcision was disgusting and the ritual laws of Judaism were silly. Disagreements like these made it hard for these people to invite each other into their homes for a meal.

Wealth, social class, and education—in addition to ethnicity—had a way of dividing people. In chapters 14 and 15 of his letter, Paul exhorted the Romans to agree to disagree about anything that was not central to the gospel, and to put more effort into caring for one another than into proving that their viewpoint was right. Anybody who thought he knew more about the spiritual life than the next person had more responsibility to bear with the other, not less.

Strong: Mature in faith and knowledgeable about the Scriptures.

Welcome one another to God's glory: "Accept one another . . . to the glory of God" (NASB). God's glory is the weighty, magnificent beauty of God's presence. Those who have some experience of living in God's presence have the honor of accepting and welcoming others into that glorious presence.

Loving One Another

Overview 5 minutes

The New Testament is full of exhortations that include the phrase "one another." These "one anothers" urge us to do something with the information we have read and heard. They effectively draw a line in the dirt in front of us, inviting us to cross it and enter a new way of living. They admonish some of us to leave a flat, lifeless existence as church attenders and to become put-your-money-where-your-mouth-is disciples of Jesus.

Saint Francis of Assisi said, "Tell everyone around you of the great love of God. When all else fails, use words."

Real love costs something. I learned 21 years ago, when a few people chose to love me even though I had chosen to make myself unlovable, that their decision cost them. I have learned that when I have had to love others in our church who didn't measure up to my mental list of acceptable attributes, it has cost me. Jesus paid the ultimate price, but he invites each of us to pick up our cross and follow him.

In this session, in addition to worship and prayer, we'll look at four of the "one anothers" and see how they may give more definition to our growing sense of caring community. We will also spend some time building up our skills of noticing and encouraging one another through an exercise in active listening.

Assignment Debriefing ▼▼▼▼▼▼▼▼▼▼▼▼▼▼▼▼▼▼ 5 minutes

1. Did any of you contact the person whose name you drew at the last meeting? If so, what did you learn about them?

   This was not a one-time assignment. If you were unable to follow through, you may pursue it this week.

2. Does anyone want to praise God for something he has done this week, an answer to a prayer from our last meeting, or something new about your faith you have discovered? (Please keep prayer requests until later in the meeting.)

Beginning ▼▼▼▼▼▼▼▼▼▼▼▼▼▼▼▼▼ 15 minutes

3. If you had the power to recreate yourself, what wouldn't you change about yourself?

4. Divide the group into two-person teams. (If there is an even number of persons, the leader should participate. If there is an odd number of persons, the leader should sit out.) The purpose of this exercise is to introduce yourself to your partner, but you must accomplish this without any words. You may use visuals, pictures, signs, gestures, signals, or anything non-verbal. You may point to a wedding ring to indicate marriage, run in place to indicate you are a jogger, and so on. Allow two minutes for each person in the team.

5. Now regather as a group. Give each person one minute to state verbally what he or she was trying to communicate non-verbally.

6. How accurate were you in describing yourself? (Rate yourself on a scale of high, passable, or not very clear.)

7. How accurate were you in reading your partner's gestures? (Again rate yourself using the same scale as above.)

8. What barriers prevented you from communicating and understanding? How can you eliminate some of those barriers in normal communication in this group?

▼ ▼ ▼ ▼ ▼ ▼ ▼ ▼ ▼ ▼ ▼ ▼ ▼ ▼ ▼ ▼ ▼ ▼ ▼
The Text   5 minutes

The following are four examples of the New Testament's "one anothers," in which Jesus and Paul explain how to proclaim the gospel and, when necessary, use words.

❶ *Ask for a volunteer to read the text aloud. You may also read some or all of the reference notes on page 59.*

"A new command I give you: Love one another. As I have loved you, so you must love one another. By this all men will know that you are my disciples, if you love one another."

(John 13:34–35)

Be devoted to one another in **brotherly love**. Honor one another above yourselves.

(Romans 12:10)

55

Accept one another, then, just as Christ accepted you, **in order to bring praise to God.**

(Romans 15:7)

You, my brothers, were called to be free. But do not use your freedom to indulge the **sinful nature**; rather, serve one another in love.

(Galatians 5:13)

Understanding the Text   15 minutes

9. Why do you think the early believers were given these instructions about the "one anothers"?

☐ They were pretty selfish people.
☐ They were so busy they would forget.
☐ They usually didn't get along very well.
☐ All this "one anothering" would attract attention from outsiders.
☐ Other:

10. What does it mean . . .

☐ to love someone?

☐ to be devoted to another person?

☐ to accept another person?

11. According to Jesus and Paul, what should be our motivation for loving, honoring, accepting, and serving one another?

Applying the Text   20 minutes

12. Why do you think the "one anothers" are important to today's church?

   ❐ We are so busy we forget.
   ❐ We don't know many people in our churches.
   ❐ We need to practice this just as much today.
   ❐ We are pretty good at these, but an occasional reminder doesn't hurt.
   ❐ Other:

13. What steps can we take as a group to practice these "one anothers"?

14. Which "one another" do you need to focus on this next week? What practical step(s) can you take to make a difference in your life?

Assignment   10 minutes

While we develop habits of "one anothering" in our group, we should also take these same habits outside the group. What simple act of kindness could you as individuals or as a group offer to someone who lives in the neighborhood? Try to be sensitive to the needs of the people around you this week. The people you see in your neighborhood, at work, where you shop, or where you go for recreation would all benefit from being shown concern or care. Consider showing someone an act of unsolicited kindness. It can be as simple as carrying a heavy package, putting a quarter in an expired parking meter, or introducing yourself to an unknown neighbor.

❶ *Brainstorm for a moment on this assignment. Keep the ideas simple and directed toward an individual (or individuals) who live(s) in the immediate area.*

Personal Learning Diary
5 minutes

► What did I learn, experience, or feel in this session?

Prayer
5 minutes

Break into groups of three for group and personal prayer support. What one thing do you wish to commit to your small prayer group for accountability regarding today's session?

Reference Notes

Setting: On the last evening that Jesus spent with his disciples before his arrest and execution, he urged them to love one another.

This small group with whom he had spent the last three years of his life would become the foundation of his church.

Paul's exhortations to the Romans to accept, honor, and be devoted to one another flowed out of his extended statement of the gospel in chapters 1–11 of this letter. Romans 12:1 summed up his argument: "Therefore, I urge you, brothers, in view of God's mercy [described in the previous eleven chapters], to offer your bodies as living sacrifices. . . ." Accepting, honoring, and being devoted to one another are ways in which we offer ourselves sacrificially to God.

Paul spent several chapters of his letter to the Galatians encouraging them not to turn their life in God's Spirit into an enslavement to rules. He urged them to live in freedom. In chapter 5, however, he cautioned that true freedom was not license to indulge their whims, but rather the freedom to serve one another.

Brotherly love: Family devotion was highly valued in ancient culture; to treat a non-relative as a brother was to take that person into one's intimate circle.

Accept one another . . . in order to bring praise to God: This is the same phrase that we saw rendered as "welcome one another to God's glory" in session 5. The phrase can be understood to say either that we are to accept one another into God's glory or for God's glory.

Sinful nature: Literally, "flesh." The flesh is our lower nature of instinct and drives. If indulged and left ungoverned by the Holy Spirit, fleshly drives quickly grow and consume our lives.

Looking Outward

Overview

▼ ▼ ▼ ▼ ▼ ▼ ▼ ▼ ▼ ▼ ▼ ▼ ▼ ▼ ▼ ▼ ▼

10 minutes

❶ *Since this is the last session in this guide, you will want to finish this meeting with a sense of accomplishment and expectancy for your group's future. Though most group members will want to continue, some may not be able to do so. Therefore, it is important to review the past weeks together and to discuss the future. It would be good to talk about the next study guide you might use and the opportunity for someone to become an apprentice leader. (See the Appendix for information on apprentice leaders.)*

For any living entity to grow and sustain life, there must be a balance between reaching inward (loving yourself) and reaching outward (loving your neighbor as yourself). Otherwise, things become stagnant and life wanes. How can a group keep the balance? The answer is not easy and varies with each group. Some things are certain, however: If you spend time talking about outreach in your group, you will ensure longer life. The other certainty is that there are no guarantees for what works and what doesn't. Still, we can count on the fact that God wants community to be built more than we do. He desires life, his life, flowing in your group each week.

A group I led decided to close its doors to newcomers for awhile. We wanted to get close to one another and work on building community. Our group did grow close, and community was growing, but something was out of balance. At the end of that year, lethargy and a lack of momentum had settled in. Finally, we took an evening to discuss the past year and the next. Someone shared how a lake without an outlet becomes a stagnant lagoon, and the life that was once there begins to die. We realized that it was time to recruit some new members, and invite new life again. We began to put an empty chair in the room each time we met, and reminded one another that there was someone in our various circles of influence who would benefit from coming to our group. We did invite others—some of them came—and the group had momentum and life again.

In this final session we examine how the earliest gathering of believers in Jerusalem balanced their inward and outward focus, and discuss how we can do the same. We will then determine our plans for the future: who will remain in the group and what we will do next. We conclude with an encouragement exercise and prayer for one another.

▼▼▼▼▼▼▼▼▼▼▼▼▼▼▼▼▼▼
Assignment Debriefing   5 minutes

1. How did last week's discussion of serving someone in a simple way affect you? Was anyone able to put this into practice?

2. What can we do to remove the obstacles to outreach?

▼▼▼▼▼▼▼▼▼▼▼▼▼▼▼▼▼▼
Beginning   15 minutes

3. What is one of the most difficult choices you have had to make in your life? What factors helped you to make that choice?

4. From our time together during the past six sessions, please share one thing you learned about yourself, or from the Scriptures, regarding caring and community.

The Text ▼▼▼▼▼▼▼▼▼▼▼▼▼▼▼▼▼▼▼ 5 minutes

Sometimes the pictures drawn by the Scriptures seem idyllic and out of reach. But they are there because they are historically accurate, and because they encourage us, enlighten us, and give us goals. This description of the Jerusalem community in the months after Pentecost is one such text. Occasionally we enter into a deep relationship that matches parts of what is described here. We would do well to use this passage as a measuring stick. How much of this type of relationship are we experiencing? How can this story encourage us to develop community of this depth?

❶ *Ask for a volunteer to read the text aloud. You may also read some or all of the reference notes on pages 66-67.*

They committed themselves to **the teaching of the apostles, the life together, the common meal**, and the prayers.

Everyone around was in awe—all those **wonders and signs** done through the apostles! And all the believers lived in a wonderful harmony, holding everything in common. They sold whatever they owned and pooled their resources so that each person's need was met.

They followed a daily discipline of worship in the Temple followed by meals at home, every meal a celebration, exuberant and joyful, as they praised God. People in general liked what they saw. Every day their number grew as God added those who were saved.

(Acts 2:42-47, MSG)

Understanding the Text

5. How is the community life you have experienced in church like the picture described in this passage? How is it different?

6. Which aspects of common life in this passage served the inward needs of the group?

7. Which ones served outsiders?

8. Of the qualities of community life listed, which one would you like to experience more fully? Why?
   - ❏ the common meal
   - ❏ prayer
   - ❏ wonders and signs
   - ❏ holding everything in common
   - ❏ giving to everyone who has a need
   - ❏ meeting in the Temple (church) and in homes
   - ❏ praising God
   - ❏ attracting the good will of outsiders
   - ❏ seeing the Lord add daily to those who are saved

Applying the Text 15–30 minutes

9. How is this picture of community still a good goal for us today? How would you like this picture to shape what your group becomes?

10. What will be your immediate plans for the next couple of months?

11. This is an encouragement and praise exercise. Ask for volunteers to sit in a chair in the middle of the room. There are two rules:

   ▶ Anyone in the group can make an encouraging statement to the person sitting in the center chair, or thank God for some characteristic or growth that they have seen in the person.

   ▶ The recipient of the encouragement, sitting in the center chair, is not allowed to say anything in response to the encouragement except, "Thank you."

Personal Learning Diary 5 minutes

   ▶ What did I learn, experience, or feel?

Prayer 5 minutes

Although you have already done some praying together during your encouragement exercise, close by praying for any remaining requests.

Reference Notes

Setting: For forty days after Jesus' resurrection, he appeared to various groups of his followers. On the fortieth day he returned to his Father. Ten days later, on the Jewish festival of Pentecost, the Holy Spirit descended upon the believers with power. About three thousand people who had come to Jerusalem for the festival were baptized after the apostle Peter preached on that day. The passage in this session immediately follows the account of what happened at Pentecost.

The teaching of the apostles: At this point all eleven of the original apostles (minus Judas, who had committed suicide) were living in Jerusalem. Apostle (literally, "one who is sent") was a Jewish term for a legal representative, someone who could agree on a contract on someone else's behalf or even stand in for the groom at a wedding. Jesus had been God's legal representative on earth, bringing God's message. Now that Jesus was gone, the apostles became Jesus' legal representatives to those who did not yet know him. Jesus had chosen twelve men to be his apostles and had imparted his teaching to them. They, in turn, were passing on that teaching along with their own memories of him, his death, and his resurrection.

The life together: This included, but was not limited to, the sharing of time, money, food, worship, and other experiences described in the rest of this passage. It also included the shared source of life: the Holy Spirit.

The common meal: The believers may have shared their meals as often as possible, and in them commemorated the Last Supper, which Jesus held with the apostles on the night before his death.

Wonders and signs: The book of Acts records some of these. The apostles spoke in foreign languages unknown to them (Acts 2) and healed a crippled beggar (Acts 3). The Holy Spirit struck dead two people who lied to Peter (Acts 5). Eventually crowds of people came from everywhere, bringing the sick and demon-afflicted, and all were healed (Acts 5:12-16).

Leader's Appendix

HOW TO PREPARE FOR THE GROUP

Definition of a Christian Small Group

A Christian small group is an intentional, face-to-face gathering of 5 to 13 people which meets on a regular basis for a particular purpose related to the members' spiritual journey.[1]

> ▶ *Christian:* Small groups meet for a variety of purposes: conversation, support, book studies, sports interests, and so on. A Christian small group meets for the purpose of knowing and following Jesus Christ.

> ▶ *Small group:* A particular relational format, different from casual conversation and different from lecture. It is a guided conversation between members of a group in which everyone can participate.

> ▶ *Intentional:* Not an accidental or ad hoc gathering of people, but one planned for a particular purpose.

> ▶ *Face-to-face:* At the heart of the small group are the interpersonal relationships between the various group members. Face-to-face communication is distinct from a classroom setting, for example.

> ▶ *5 to 13:* With fewer than five members, it is hard to sustain the intentional aspect of the dialogue, and so the small group becomes a conversation between three or four friends. (The exception is when subgroups are

formed from a larger small group for certain exercises.) When you have more than 13 people, it is easy for some members to disengage from the dialogue, so the group becomes more like an interactive lecture with only a few people who participate.

▶ *Regular:* This is part of the intentionality of a small group. It has an agreed-upon time schedule. Once a week is the optimum schedule, but small groups can function on a biweekly or even monthly basis.

▶ *Particular purpose:* The small group comes together to accomplish a particular task, study particular material, or relate in a particular way. The aims and goals of the small group are defined by the covenant (or ground rules) worked out among the members.

▶ *Spiritual journey:* In the end, the aim of the small group is to help all members know and follow Jesus more consistently in whatever place God has put them (or they find themselves), and to whatever end God has for them.

Establishing the Purpose of Your Group

Can't we just get together and have fun? Of course you can, but unless you first discuss your assumptions with each other, you will find later on that people have differing perspectives on where your group is supposed to be going and how it should get there. Everyone has an unspoken agenda and goal in mind. The first step is to talk about those assumptions openly, and if you are so inclined, to write down a common purpose statement. A purpose statement is no more than a sentence or two describing who you are as a group and why you meet. For example:

> *The Parents of Teens Group exists to provide a venue to discuss issues related to parenting adolescents and to develop a place for mutual care, encouragement, and growth for the group members and guests.*

By working through this exercise together, you will discover common goals as well as differences in expectations. Taking the time to establish common ground will help lay the foundation for community, mutual respect, and honest discussion. You can shape your purpose statement along with your group covenant in session 4.

Optimum Size of the Group

Group size is at its optimum or maximum when it matches the ability of the leader's (and apprentice leader's) ability to adequately care for the group members. There is no magic number, but it is generally accepted that the average lay leader can care adequately for five or six people. Therefore, a leader with an apprentice can lead a group of ten to twelve in regular attendance. Once the group is larger than that on a regular basis, group dynamics change and the dominant personalities will tend to control the discussion and sharing times.

If you find yourself in a group that has grown large, you can still offer a comfortable place for people to share their lives and prayers if you ask them to form sub-groups; that is, to break down into groups of three to four (never more than five) for discussion and prayer. Check with the host or hostess for separate areas of the house where sub-groups may go for confidentiality and ease of hearing.

Meeting Places

A group can meet anywhere a safe, warm atmosphere can be developed. Groups can work well in any venue as long as the host or hostess has put some forethought into the user-friendliness of the meeting place. We have done successful groups in government buildings simply by arranging the meeting room to accommodate the group. Generally, homes work better than other facilities because they lend themselves to a comfortable atmosphere. Church facilities often work best for support or recovery groups that deal with difficult personal issues. They offer an anonymous atmosphere many people need when beginning to deal with their issues. Issues to consider include:

- ► Is the location easily accessible?
- ► Is there adequate parking?
- ► Are there stairs or other impediments that might prevent someone from attending?
- ► Does the host or hostess have pets?
- ► How does the host or hostess feel about having a group in the house every week for six to twelve months?
- ► Does the location have adequate space for children?
- ► If in an apartment/condo/townhouse, what is the noise level from adjoining units?
- ► Is there adequate room for the group to break into sub-groups for discussion and prayer?

Room Setup

Room setup is a significant factor in determining the friendliness of a meeting. Consider these questions:

> ► Can the room be set up so that everyone is facing each other?
> ► Is the room large enough to accommodate ten to twelve people comfortably?
> ► Can everyone in the room make eye contact? (It is important that everyone is face-to-face and not in the second row or in back of another participant.)
> ► Is the room free from distractions?

How Often, How Long

A group gels most quickly and develops into a caring community best when it meets every week. Groups can meet twice a month or even monthly (although this is not suggested since it lessens caring) if they meet weekly for the first six to eight weeks to establish a foundation for the group. A group develops much more quickly (almost exponentially) when there is weekly group contact and between-meeting contact among group members.

Your meeting will generally work best when it is between ninety minutes and two hours in length. Some groups work well at one hour, especially if they are constrained by a lunch hour or other scheduling issues.

Groups should begin and end on time. You honor the group members by keeping on schedule. Do not allow a habitual latecomer to determine the starting time. Many groups work well with a soft and hard closing time. For example, if your group meets from 7:00 to 8:30, announce that the meeting is officially done at 8:30, so that those who need to leave may do so (the soft finish). The others in the group may stay to socialize if the host agrees. The meeting should then finish and all should leave at an agreed-upon time (the hard finish).

Whom to Invite

Take the attitude that everyone would benefit from being in a group. This attitude will allow you to view everyone as a potential group member. Use your five circles of influence to recruit from:

> ► Family
> ► Friends

- ► Neighbors
- ► Coworkers
- ► Fellow Churchgoers

A Successful First Meeting: Pray, Plan, Recruit

The first meeting often sets the tone for the group, so it is very important.

Your most important job is to pray and remind yourself that you are in partnership with God. As you are connected with him in prayer and are refreshed by him, you will have something significant to offer the group.

Next, relax. You probably have much higher expectations of your leadership than anyone else in the group.

Prepare. Know what you intend to do, and in a general sense, what you want to convey to the group. Don't get caught in the trap of having a rigid agenda.

Spend some time with your host or hostess ahead of time. Find out what his or her expectations are, and share your general agenda and time schedule. Determine what the hosts are comfortable with regarding how long group members may stay, any off-limit areas of the home, and so on. If you set house rules for the group or ask the host to do so, you will head off possible misunderstandings and problems later on.

Recruit, recruit, recruit. Ask everyone to come to your group. If you are not sold on the idea that this will be a great group (with potential for friendships, mutual care, and learning) then you cannot expect others to be too enthusiastic. Again, using the diagram of your areas of influence, review the names of those in your life who could benefit from being in a warm, caring, supportive, relevant group. Pray for those on your list, and then invite them. Remember, an answer of "I don't know" or "maybe" is not a "no." Often people need some time to think about the idea. Give them a few days or a week, and extend the invitation again.

Finally, remember that God wants you to succeed in leading this group, and he loves these people more than you do. Prepare, pray, and then go in his strength and the confidence you have in his ability to mold your members into a loving group.

FACILITATING WORSHIP IN A SMALL GROUP[2]

The small group offers an environment where individuals can learn to worship God while they learn to interact with other worshipers. The key issues in leading worship in a group turning our thoughts and attention totally to God, and being honest—letting him know how much we love and adore him for who he is. If people are encouraged and led (not driven) into worship, they will grow in confidence and ability. They will learn the delicate balance between focusing on God our Father and being aware of other worshipers. These skills, which can help you maintain balance and order, can then be used in the congregational setting as well as private worship.

There are a number of useful ways to include worship in your group. You could assign your apprentice or someone else in the group the task of planning worship for each meeting.

Using the Psalms for Personal and Group Worship

The Psalms are a beautiful and personal collection of the very heartbeat of King David and other psalmists. The language of *The Message: Psalms* is down-to-earth and allows you to experience the emotions of the author. The Psalms stir our hearts, make us more vulnerable to God, and lead us into more intimate communication with him.

Read a section of the Psalms. Take time to meditate on that section and then on each verse. Let the tone, the emotion, the intensity, and the intimacy expressed by the author influence your thinking and touch your heart. If you find this type of worship exercise helpful, you might buy several paperback copies of *The Message: Psalms* for group members to share during worship. You can select one or more psalms for the group to read together and meditate on.

Try varying the way in which you read the psalm. You could have someone read one verse at a time, pausing between verses to allow the group to think about each verse silently. You could read the psalm in unison, or have sub-groups read the verses alternately.

A Capella Singing as Worship

If no one plays an instrument, the group may sing *a capella* (without instruments). There should be one person who leads, initiates, and determines the direction and duration of each song, and the entire portion of worship in song. In rare instances, a group may allow various individuals to initiate songs at random, with the group joining in spontaneously. The risk in this is that the group may end up singing the old favorites of the most vocal person, rather than a flow of worship

74

led by the Spirit of God. It's very important that the leader is wise and gentle, able to discern and guide the group through the possible pitfalls of this approach.

Using a Guitar, Piano, Keyboard, or Recording to Lead Worship

The worship leader does not have to play an instrument but should be the one who selects, begins, and ends the songs. When possible, there should be a person who plays an instrument (such as guitar or keyboard) and who also sings. He or she may be accompanied by other players and singers. The worship leader also needs to work closely with the group leader, to coordinate with the leader's plans for the group, and to adjust the length and mood of worship to complement the group agenda. In many groups where a worship leader is active, the worship leader is seen as part of the group leader team.

When choosing songs for group worship, attention should be given to a flow in the songs. Worship is often broken into two parts: worship songs that focus on who God is, and praise songs that focus on what God does.

Many groups have had success in using prerecorded worship songs. There are quite a few available today that can work well in almost every setting. The important thing is to have an environment of willingness to worship and surrender to God, no matter what musical means are employed.

Using Silence and Meditation as Worship

It is important to use silence and meditation as part of your group worship. The *selah* or pause that is injected throughout the Psalms is a good cue for us to take a few moments and quietly reflect. Meditation (being silent and thinking about what you have just read or heard) is good for the group, and a discipline that we do not practice enough.

Reading or Quoting Favorite Scriptures

Scripture reading as a part of worship can be effective in directing the group's attention to God and his desire to be in communion with us. When people who have come from busy schedules (at home and work) hear the Word proclaimed and are encouraged to meditate on it, their attention and focus can be directed from their circumstances to our awesome and holy God!

RECRUITING AN APPRENTICE

Why Have an Apprentice?

God's plan is to call all men and women and ask everyone to put their hand to the plow: "Jesus said, 'No procrastination. No backward looks. You can't put God's kingdom off till tomorrow. Seize the day'" (Luke 9:62, MSG).

Two things in the life of a healthy small group are generally necessary and predictable. One is that the group will attract and add new members. As the members of the group begin to take ownership, they will want to invite friends, fellow workers, fellow churchgoers, and family members to come and see what's happening. Consequently, the small group will grow and eventually become a large group. However, an effective group should not grow much past ten to twelve regular attendees. We know that an average layperson leading a group will be able to adequately care for about five people, so with a group of ten there are already people who may not be receiving care and follow-up. Therefore, the second necessary fact of group life has already come into play, that of leadership multiplication, or what is currently termed "apprentice leader development." It is a natural part of every healthy life to grow, multiply or divide, and grow some more. Such is the case with normal, healthy small groups.

If your group follows this natural course, it only makes sense to plan for it and participate in the process. Planning should encompass several questions:

- ▶ Who can lead?
- ▶ How do I recruit someone?
- ▶ How soon do I recruit an apprentice?
- ▶ How do I begin to develop this person into an apprentice leader?

Whom to Recruit

Apprentice-making is best worked out through prayer and wise counsel. Check with your pastor and/or small group coordinator. Get some help in selecting a person who is interested in serving and praying for other members of the group. Leadership is never lording over others or simply showing up and directing a meeting. Rather, it is fulfilling God's plan for all his daughters and sons to be cared for and assisted along the way toward him. The best leaders are generally the best servants. Look for persons who enjoy serving and helping, who have:

- ▶ a searching mind
- ▶ a humble heart
- ▶ an evident gift
- ▶ a faithful spirit

Spend time with them. Light their fire. People are already motivated by God—tap into that!

- ▶ Tell them your vision of their potential.
- ▶ Share your commitment to their development.
- ▶ Provide them with a specific assignment: "He who is faithful with little things will be faithful in big things."
- ▶ Let them pray about the opportunity.
- ▶ If they say yes, give them a job description[3] and involve them in ministry.
- ▶ If they say no, observe them for a period of time and approach them again.

When you recruit apprentice leaders, look for Davids for leadership—people who at first glance are not obvious leaders. We tend to look for the person who is naturally talented or a manager in business. God knew this and intervened through the prophet Samuel when he was sent to anoint the next king:

> But the Lord said to Samuel, "Do not consider his appearance or his height, for I have rejected him. The Lord does not look at the things man looks at. Man looks at the outward appearance, but the Lord looks at the heart."
>
> (1 Samuel 16:7)

This amazing act of divine intervention expressed God's wisdom and compassion. God knew even Samuel would tend to go to the oldest, best-looking son. But God had Samuel look at each of the sons and hear God say "not this one," until David was sent for and received the Lord's approval.

Jesus also gave us guidelines to follow in selecting leaders and apprentices. He said the people were like sheep without a shepherd (Matthew 9:36) and commanded his disciples to pray for workers for the harvest. The disciples were the answer to the prayer. The call to the disciples is the call to us, and Jesus' model is instructive: He started with them as workers. They were not hired; they were developed and empowered. Only after several years were they released and deployed as leaders.

Raising up apprentice leaders will at times be irritating and difficult. It takes time, energy, and resources, somewhat like training little children. They are interested, exuberant, and sometimes motivated. But often in attempting to do a task for the first time, they miss the mark and get discouraged. We have a great opportunity and responsibility to remind them that failure is always a step in the right direction, if we learn from it. No one does it completely right on the first attempt. Don't wait until they have done it 100 percent right to praise them. Praise any right step toward the goal.

---

1 This definition is a reworking of a classic statement by Dr. Roberta Hestenes.

2 Adapted from *The Worship Manual* by Danny Daniels.

3 *The Small Group Fitness Kit,* also by Thom Corrigan (NavPress, 1996), gives a sample job description for an apprentice leader.

Phone List

Name / Address / Phone

Turn your group into a community.

Most study guides are designed for individual use. While packed with good material, they don't provide much help in the way of group dynamic.

That's where PILGRIMAGE study guides are different. By incorporating community-building questions and exercises into each session, PILGRIMAGE guides will help your group grow closer relationally as you grow deeper spiritually. THE PILGRIMAGE SERIES includes titles like:

Seven Traits of a Successful Leader
by Jeff Arnold

Whether you're teaching a class or leading a group, there are certain character qualities that can significantly increase your impact. This guide will help you develop the seven essential traits of a successful leader.
(ISBN: 1-57683-019-5; 7 sessions; 96 pages)

Seven Tools for Building Effective Groups
by Jeff Arnold

Just as the most talented carpenter would be handicapped without the right tools, there are key skills every effective group leader must possess. This guide features the seven most important.
(ISBN: 1-57683-020-9; 7 sessions; 96 pages)

What We Believe
by Jeff Arnold

Of all the doctrines and versions of Christianity in circulation today, which ones are non-negotiable? Drawn from the Apostles' Creed, *What We Believe* examines the age old core beliefs of the Faith.
(ISBN: 1-57683-071-3; 8 sessions; 80 pages)

101 Great Ideas to Create a Caring Group
by Thom Corrigan

Many believe the single highest felt need in our society is the need to belong. To know someone else cares about us. Here are 101 tried and true ideas for cultivating an atmosphere of care in any small group.
(ISBN: 1-57683-072-1; 80 pages)

These and other NavPress study guides are available at your local Christian bookstore. Or call 1-800-366-7788 to order.

NAVPRESS
BRINGING TRUTH TO LIFE